C O N T E M P O R A

Breakthroughs

Science

CONTEMPORARY'S

Breakthroughs

in Science

EXERCISE BOOK

McGraw Hill Wright Group

 **Wright Group**

ISBN: 0-8092-3289-8

Send all inquiries to:
Wright Group/McGraw-Hill
130 East Randolph Street, Suite 400
Chicago, Illinois 60601

Printed in the United States of America.

 9 10 VLP VLP 08 07 06

The *McGraw·Hill* Companies

CONTENTS

Evaluating Ideas

TO THE STUDENT

Welcome to the *Breakthroughs in Science Exercise Book*. In this book, you'll be practicing the skills you learned in Contemporary's *Breakthroughs in Science*. You will practice how to read passages as well as illustrations such as charts, graphs, and diagrams.

Each exercise in this book corresponds to one or more lessons in *Breakthrougs in Science*. Look for the words "Text Pages" in the margin of each exercise. They will tell you where to learn more about that skill in the Breakthroughs book.

At the back of the book, you'll find answers to all the exercises. Be sure to check your work at the end of each exercise before you move on. When you are asked to write an answer, answer fully in your own words. Writing is a very important part of learning. Don't worry about your handwriting, grammar, or spelling. Getting your ideas on paper is what counts.

When you are finished with the exercises, take the Post-Test. A chart on page 64 will help you evaluate the work you have done.

And finally, read beyond the pages of this book. Read newspapers, magazines, road maps, and anything else you can get your hands on. Reading will help you prepare not only for academic work but also for the rest of your life.

THE SCIENTIFIC METHOD

TEXT PAGES
17–18

Fact and Opinion

A *fact* is a statement that can be proved by observation or measurement. For example, moonlight is reflected sunlight. An *opinion* is a personal belief that depends on your values and cannot be proved. For example, watermelon tastes better than grapes. While opinions are important in guiding scientists, it is the discovery of scientific facts that leads to scientific progress. Advances in technology, health care, and understanding our world depend on uncovering scientific facts. This is why it is important for you to know the difference between fact and opinion.

Directions: Write *F* before the statements that are facts (that can be proved by observation or measurement) and *O* before the statements that are opinions (that depend on a person's values).

EXAMPLES

_F_ Ninety percent of all divorced people say they feel depressed.

_O_ Divorce is a terrible experience.

_____ **1.** Daily exercise can lower many people's blood pressure.

_____ **2.** All people over the age of 60 should exercise.

_____ **3.** Real whipped cream tastes better than artificial whipped cream.

_____ **4.** Seventy percent of all American children believe in Santa Claus.

_____ **5.** Last night we got a record 3.6 inches of rain.

_____ **6.** Rain always brings good luck.

_____ **7.** The *Voyager 2* mission led to the discovery of rings around the planet Jupiter.

_____ **8.** Jupiter's rings are the most beautiful sight in our solar system.

Check your answers on page 66.

Everyday Hypotheses

A *hypothesis* is a reasonable explanation of observed facts. Scientists look at the facts of a problem and then make an educated guess to explain these facts.

Directions: After reading each of the everyday situations below, write a hypothesis to explain each set of facts.

EXAMPLE

You notice a puddle of oil on the garage floor under your car. You check the oil level in your car's engine and find it is lower than usual.

What is your hypothesis? *Oil is leaking from the engine.*

1. The leaves on one of your houseplants are turning yellow. The plant gets plenty of sunlight and water, but it is located in front of a drafty window where it gets very cold.

   What is your hypothesis? _____

2. One day at the train station, you notice the time on your watch is later than the time on the station clock. You reset your watch to the time on the station clock, but the next day your watch is ahead of the station clock again. The conductor assures you the station clock is correct.

   What is your hypothesis? _____

3. Your neighbor has gone on vacation for seven days, but you don't know when he left. On Friday, a friend of your neighbor asks you when the neighbor will be back. You notice four newspapers in the hallway outside his door, one for Tuesday, Wednesday, Thursday, and Friday.

   What is your hypothesis? _____

4. Mary works for a company that removes asbestos, a cancer-causing agent, from old buildings. She tests the air several times each day to see if asbestos particles are present. On the first day of a job, before the workers showed up in the morning, Mary tested the air and found no trace of asbestos. Later that day, when the workers were removing the floor tiles, she ran a second test and found slight traces of asbestos. When the workers began removing the ceiling tiles, Mary tested the air again and found very high levels of asbestos. She wrote down her hypothesis about where the asbestos was coming from.

   What is your hypothesis? _____

Check your answers on page 66.

Choosing Hypotheses

Directions: Read the situations below, and circle the hypothesis that best explains each set of facts.

1. In 1928, British scientist Alexander Fleming made a hypothesis that led to the discovery of penicillin. He found *penicillium* mold growing in a lab dish and noticed that all the bacteria around the mold had died. When he mixed the mold into a liquid, he found that no bacteria grew in the liquid. His hypothesis was that

   (1) bacteria and penicillium mold can live together

   (2) penicillium mold destroys all living things

   (3) penicillium mold cannot be mixed with liquids

   (4) bacteria can grow in laboratory dishes but not in liquids

   (5) penicillium mold kills bacteria

2. A doctor examined a group of four tourists. Three of them had gotten sick after eating at a restaurant. He suspected food poisoning, so he asked them about their symptoms and what they had eaten for dinner.

	Food	**Symptoms**
Tourist #1:	Cheese and crackers, chicken salad, pork chops, green beans, baked potato with butter, ice cream	Nausea, vomiting
Tourist #2:	Bread and cheese, lettuce salad with dressing, tomato soup, steak, baked potato with sour cream, green beans, and apple pie	None
Tourist #3:	Cheese and crackers, lettuce salad with tomatoes and dressing, chicken salad sandwich, french fries	Nausea, vomiting
Tourist #4:	Crackers with butter, chicken salad, grilled ham and cheese sandwich, french fries	Nausea, vomiting

   The doctor most likely hypothesized that the illness was caused by

   (1) butter

   (2) lettuce

   (3) chicken salad

   (4) ice cream

   (5) cheese

Check your answers on page 66.

Making Hypotheses

Directions: Write your own scientific hypotheses to fit the following situations.

1. Angela Ford was stringing Christmas tree lights. She knew that since the bulbs are run in sequence, none of them would light if there were any bad bulbs on the string. When she plugged in the string, none of the lights went on. What was Angela's hypothesis about why the lights wouldn't work?

   _____

2. Angela examined the string and found one bulb that looked black and burned. She replaced the black bulb with a spare bulb that came with the lights. Since the spare bulb came with the set, she assumed it was good and did not test it. When she plugged in the string with the spare light bulb, the lights still did not go on. What new hypothesis can explain this observation?

   _____

3. Angela decided to test the spare bulb. She had a second string of lights that worked, so she knew all the bulbs were good. She removed one of the bulbs on the second string and inserted the spare bulb. The lights went on. What did Angela learn about the spare bulb?

   _____

4. She removed the spare bulb from the second string and replaced it with the black bulb from the first string. The lights did not go on. What did she learn about the black bulb?

   _____

5. She went back to the first string and inserted the spare bulb where the black bulb had been. The lights still did not go on. She knew that the electric socket was good, so what was her hypothesis about why the lights didn't work?

   _____

6. How could Angela test the lights on the first string?

   _____

   _____

Check your answers on page 66.

Errors in Experiments _____

After making a hypothesis, scientists test it by performing an *experiment*. They use *subjects* (such as mice) as the experimental group. Other subjects, not experimented on, act as the *control group*. *Conditions* (such as the amount of food or exercise) must be kept the same, except for the variable being tested.

Directions: Tell what is wrong with each of these experiments. Choose from the list below.

- **subjects not similar**
- **conditions not kept the same**
- **no control group**
- **not enough subjects**

1. Chin-Hwa decided to do an experiment to see if mice could tell the difference between colors. He put several mice in a box with three doors—a blue door, a green door, and a red door—and put a dish of food behind the green door each day. At first, the mice looked behind all the doors for food. But after two weeks, they went straight to the green door. Chin-Hwa concluded that mice can see colors.

   What's wrong? _____

2. Imelda wanted to see if a new toothpaste prevented cavities better than regular toothpaste. She gave it to her daughter Marie. She let another daughter, Anita, brush with regular toothpaste. After three months, Anita had two new cavities and Marie had none. Imelda concluded the new toothpaste was better at stopping cavities.

   What's wrong? _____

3. When Ernest bought a new pickup truck, he decided to try snow tires. His old car, a small two-door, never had snow tires, and it slid all over the road when it snowed. Ernest put the snow tires on his truck and found he had much better traction than he did with the two-door. He concluded that snow tires are good for gaining traction.

   What's wrong? _____

4. Carmen decided to test a new laundry detergent to see if it got her clothes cleaner. She washed a load of whites with her old detergent in hot water. She washed another load of whites with the new detergent in cold water. She then compared the two loads. The load washed in hot water was much cleaner than the one washed in cold water. Carmen concluded that the new detergent was not as good as her old detergent.

   What's wrong? _____

Check your answers on page 66.

Review of the Scientific Method _____

Directions: The phrases on the left describe each step of the scientific method. The sentences on the right describe how one scientist developed a theory. Match each step of the scientific method with the corresponding step of the theory development.

_____ 1. asking the right question

_____ 2. collecting the facts

_____ 3. making a hypothesis

_____ 4. testing the hypothesis

_____ 5. deciding on a theory

a. A sixteenth-century astronomer named Nicolaus Copernicus wondered whether the common belief that the Earth was the center of the universe was correct.

b. Copernicus guessed that the sun and the other planets do not rotate around the Earth.

c. He compared his guess to the data he collected about the other planets.

d. He studied and recorded the movement of the other planets.

e. He decided that the Earth and the other planets rotate around the sun.

Check your answers on page 67.

UNDERSTANDING WHAT YOU READ

TEXT PAGES
28–30

Restating Facts

Restating facts is simply a matter of saying the same thing in different words. The ability to restate facts can help you make sure you understand the material you read. It can also help you answer test questions, since test writers often restate in the questions what you've read in a passage.

Directions: Read each of the sentences below and circle the number of the answer that best restates the facts.

1. Without computers, space travel would be impossible.

    (1) Computers make it possible to do great things.

    (2) Nobody thought of traveling in space before computers.

    (3) Computers make space travel possible.

    (4) Computers open new doors for the human race.

    (5) Astronauts must understand a great deal about computers.

2. When the supply of energy and water to corn plants is increased, the plants' rate of growth increases as well.

    (1) The more sun and water a corn plant gets, the faster it will grow.

    (2) Without energy and water, corn plants will die.

    (3) Corn plants grow bigger when they get more water.

    (4) Today, corn plants get more energy and water than ever before.

    (5) Water and sunlight greatly accelerate the process of photosynthesis.

3. Although nuclear power presents many problems for society, it provides much of the electricity that we use in our daily lives.

    (1) Nuclear power has more drawbacks than other methods of generating electricity.

    (2) We will soon have to use nuclear power whether we like it or not.

    (3) Few people understand what nuclear power is all about.

    (4) Although it's not perfect, nuclear power is a necessary part of our lives.

    (5) Nuclear power is one of life's many drawbacks.

Check your answers on page 67.

Restating Practice

Directions: After reading each of the sentences below, restate the facts using your own words.

EXAMPLE

A diet high in fat increases the risk of heart disease.

If you eat a lot of fatty foods, you are more likely to have heart disease.

1. Atoms are the building blocks of all matter.

   _____

2. The United States is the world's number-one consumer of gasoline.

   _____

3. Even today, the reason for the dinosaurs' extinction remains a mystery to scientists.

   _____

4. The world's oldest living tree first took root about 4,600 years ago.

   _____

5. Strong evidence suggests that alcoholism may be an inherited trait.

   _____

6. One example of the intelligence of porpoises is their ability to cooperate with and protect each other in varying environmental circumstances.

   _____

   _____

7. Despite the greater size and speed of modern football players, football is less dangerous today than it was 50 years ago.

   _____

   _____

8. Computer literacy is a valuable asset in today's workplace.

   _____

Check your answers on page 67.

Summarizing Facts

To *summarize* means to put all the important facts together in one short statement.

Directions: Read each group of facts. Then circle the best summary.

1. The bubonic plague is one of the deadliest diseases we know.

   From 1348 to 1400, outbreaks of the plague killed more than one-third of Europe's population.

   The plague, spread by rat fleas, was deadliest in towns where rats were numerous and where people lived close together.

   Violent outbreaks of the plague continued into the early 1900s.

   Today, the plague is rare and can be treated with antibiotics.

   What is the best summary of these facts?

   (1) The bubonic plague is a very deadly disease.

   (2) The plague is spread by rat fleas.

   (3) Although the bubonic plague did most of its damage in the 1300s, it continued to ravage the population for centuries.

   (4) The bubonic plague, once the most deadly disease in the world, is almost nonexistent today.

2. Acid rain occurs when rain "moves" pollutants from the air and carries them into lakes, streams, and forests.

   Acid rain pollutes lakes and streams, killing fish and animals.

   Forests suffer from acid rain because it kills trees and plants.

   Many scientists believe much of the acid rain that falls in Canada is caused by air pollution from U.S. factories.

   This issue has strained relations between our country and Canada.

   What is the best summary of these facts?

   (1) Acid rain destroys plants and animals.

   (2) Scientists disagree on what causes acid rain.

   (3) Acid rain hurts both our environment and our relations with Canada.

   (4) Acid rain helps keep the air clean.

Check your answers on page 67.

Summarizing Practice _____

Directions: After carefully reading each group of facts, summarize them using your own words.

EXAMPLE

The weather was perfect for the company picnic.

Everybody ate lots of food.

We played softball until it was too dark to see.

After sunset, we laughed and sang for hours.

SUMMARY: *Everyone had fun at the company picnic.* _____

1. Pocket calculators that cost $10 today were very expensive when they were first introduced to the public.

   When compact disc players were first released, they were three to four times more expensive than they are today.

   A $10,000 computer of ten years ago can't do nearly as much as a $2,000 computer can today.

   Walkman-type stereos can be bought today for a fraction of their original selling prices.

   SUMMARY: _____

2. Computers can handle information faster and more efficiently than humans can.

   Before computers do work, programmers "tell" them what to do.

   A computer cannot perform a task if it has not been programmed to do so.

   So far, no one has found a way for computers to make their own decisions and value judgments.

   SUMMARY: _____

3. Fuels are substances that can be burned to produce heat or power.

   Fossil fuels, such as coal, petroleum, and natural gas, are the most widely used fuels.

   The earth has a limited supply of fossil fuels.

   Scientists are developing ways to use other power sources, such as the wind and solar radiation.

   SUMMARY: _____

Check your answers on page 67.

Main Idea of a Paragraph _____

The *main idea* is the most important point an author is trying to make in a paragraph or passage. The rest of the paragraph or passage is filled with *details* that explain or prove the main idea.

Directions: Underline the sentence that states the main idea of each paragraph.

EXAMPLE

From 7 o'clock that morning until 11 o'clock the next night, the snow continued to fall. The heavy snowfall caused many problems. Traffic came to a standstill as drivers abandoned their cars in deep snowdrifts. School closings were announced all over the northern part of the state. Trains ran hours behind schedule when they ran at all, and tens of thousands of people found it impossible to get to work. Stores, restaurants, and theaters stood quiet and empty. By the time the snow stopped falling, all business had ground to a halt.

The main idea is in the second sentence, *The heavy snowfall caused many problems.* The rest of the paragraph contains details that support the main idea.

1. Although people think of fat as unhealthy, most wild animals cannot do without it. Fat can be very important to the survival of animals. In very cold climates, for example, fat helps animals stay warm by providing a layer of insulation just beneath the skin. Since fat is lighter than water, it also helps marine animals to stay afloat and move around in the water. When animals such as hedgehogs hibernate in the winter, fat provides the food they need until spring. Their bodies turn the excess fat into energy.

2. We have uncovered many mysteries about the relationship between the brain and the body. We know that people can control their heartbeat by concentration. We know that stress—the reaction of our bodies to outside events—is caused by how the mind sees the outside world. We have even recorded strange patterns of brain waves in sleeping people. Apparently, the brain has something to do with re-energizing our bodies. But while we know a great deal about *what* the brain does, we know far less about *how* it does it.

3. While birds and mammals are similar in some ways, their differences help them adapt to different environments. Birds—warm-blooded animals with feathers—grind their food in their gizzards to help digestion. Most mammals—warm-blooded animals with hair or fur—chew their food with their teeth. The brains of birds are small in proportion to the rest of their bodies; the brains of mammals are proportionally larger. Birds have hollow bones, which makes them light and helps them to fly. The bones of mammals are solid and much better suited to the challenge of life on the ground.

4. Before Charles Darwin published his book *The Origin of Species*, many people believed in the Bible's explanation of how humans were created. In his book, Darwin claimed that humans had descended not from Adam and Eve but from lower primates that resembled the great apes of today. The book caused outrage around the world. Religious leaders burned it in the streets. Even today, although many of Darwin's theories are supported by scientific evidence, people still argue about the theory of evolution. Darwin's book was—and still is—a very controversial work.

5. Researchers have often asked, "Were we born to be certain kinds of people, or does our environment shape us into the people we are?" One possible answer lies in the study of identical twins. Identical twins offer scientists a unique opportunity to compare the effects of heredity and environment. Since identical twins share identical genes, they are "born to be" the exact same person. The reason they're not, of course, is that their individual life experiences affect and shape their personalities. So when researchers compare the personalities of twins, they know that the differences between them are largely the result of differing environments.

Check your answers on pages 67-68.

Main Idea of a Passage

Finding the main idea of a passage is much like finding the main idea of a paragraph. By looking at the main idea of each paragraph, you can tell what the passage is about.

Directions: Read the passage and answer the questions in your own words.

Monkey Talk

We humans have always thought we were the only animals able to learn a language. Language has given us the power to explore ideas. It has allowed us to build great societies. It has enabled us to record our thoughts and experiences for future generations. Language, we have always believed, sets us apart from other animals.

---

1. What is the main idea of the paragraph above?

_____

Then came Washoe. Washoe was a chimpanzee who learned to speak with American sign language, a system of hand movements representing different words and ideas. For five years, Washoe stayed with Allen and Trixie Gardner, two psychology professors at the University of Nevada. During that time, Washoe learned to use more than 130 different hand signals. She learned to identify simple objects such as a toothbrush and an apple. She learned to express simple concepts like "open" and "sweet." She learned to string words together into correct sentences, making statements and observations, asking questions, and even talking to herself!

---

2. What is the main idea of the paragraph above?

_____

The Washoe experiments have helped us to understand what happens when people (or chimpanzees) learn to use language. They've taught us to recognize different types of intelligence in animals. But most important, Washoe has disproved the idea that humans are the only animals capable of using language. We now understand that we share some very important abilities with other species. And we have begun to rethink what it means to be human.

---

3. What is the main idea of the last paragraph on page 14?

_____

4. Write a one-sentence summary of the three main ideas from the previous passage.

_____

_____

5. Which of the following conclusions can you draw from the passage? Put a check (✔) next to each correct answer.

_____ **a.** Dolphins might also be capable of learning a language.

_____ **b.** Without language, humans could never have built great cities.

_____ **c.** Humans still have a lot to learn about the English language.

_____ **d.** Chimpanzees are more like humans than we thought.

_____ **e.** Washoe is probably the smartest chimpanzee that ever lived.

6. Which of the following is _not_ discussed in the passage?

(1) Washoe's daily life in Africa

(2) the importance of language in passing along history

(3) the ability of animals to learn language

(4) the assumptions humans make about themselves

(5) Washoe's ability to make sentences

7. What is the main idea of the passage?

(1) Animals are capable of learning a language.

(2) Chimpanzees can learn to "speak" as well as humans.

(3) By learning to use language, Washoe changed the way humans think of themselves.

(4) Washoe has proved that chimpanzees are as skilled with language as humans.

(5) Human beings are no longer superior to animals.

Your answer for question 4 should be almost the same as your answer for question 7. If your answers are very different, reread the passage and think again about the main ideas.

Check your answers on page 68.

UNDERSTANDING ILLUSTRATIONS

TEXT PAGES
57–59

Diagrams

A *diagram* is a drawing that shows the parts of something and how it works. When reading a diagram, always look at the *title* and the *labels*.

Directions: Look over each diagram and answer the questions that follow.

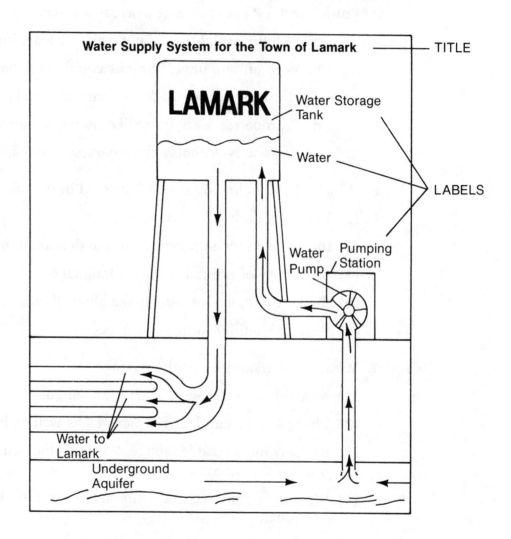

1. What is the title of the diagram?

_____

2. Where is the water pump located?

_____

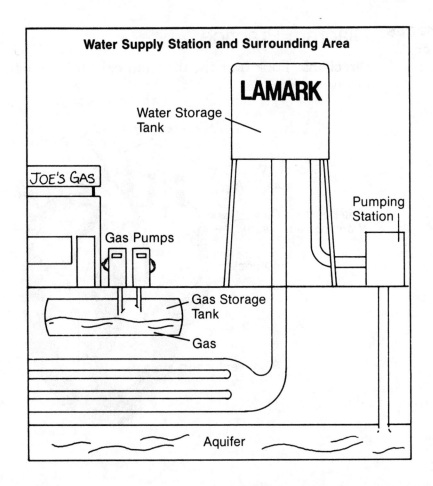

Water Supply Station and Surrounding Area

LAMARK

Water Storage Tank

JOE'S GAS

Gas Pumps

Pumping Station

Gas Storage Tank

Gas

Aquifer

This diagram shows an expanded version of the diagram on the left. Notice the gas station next to the pumping station. Like the water supply system, the gas station system uses pumps and storage tanks.

3. According to the diagram, where is the gas stored?

_____

4. What would happen to the gasoline in the reserve tank if the bottom of the tank rusted out?

_____

5. Could a leak in the gas storage tank affect the people of Lamark? How?

_____

Check your answers on page 68.

Diagram Practice

Directions: Look over the diagram carefully and answer the questions below.

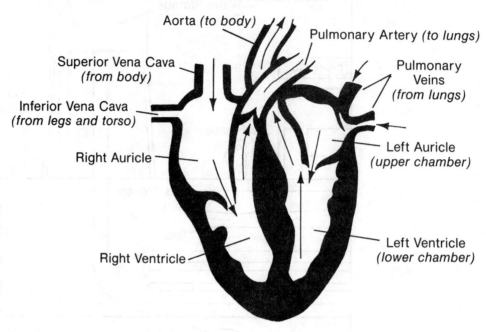

The Human Heart

1. What is the title of the diagram?

   _____

2. What are the upper chambers of the heart called?

   _____

3. Where does the blood go when it leaves the left ventricle?

   _____

4. Where does the blood go after it leaves the lungs?

   _____

5. The blood that is pumped to the body from the aorta contains oxygen. The blood returning to the heart from the superior vena cava has much less. Based on the information in the diagram, where do you think the blood gets its fresh supply of oxygen?

   _____

Check your answers on page 68.

Comparing Diagrams

Arteries are blood vessels that carry oxygenated blood to the rest of the body. Sometimes fat builds up inside the arteries, preventing blood from flowing through them. When this happens, different parts of the body are cut off from their supply of oxygen and nutrition. A *stroke* occurs when the blood is blocked from reaching the brain. A *heart attack* occurs when the blood fails to reach the heart muscles.

Directions: Look over the diagram carefully and answer the questions below.

Cross Sections of Human Arteries
(20× larger than actual)

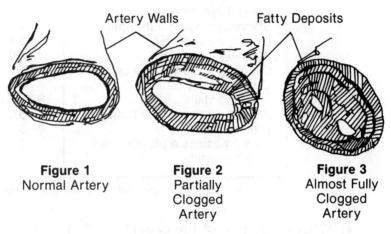

Artery Walls   Fatty Deposits

Figure 1
Normal Artery

Figure 2
Partially
Clogged
Artery

Figure 3
Almost Fully
Clogged
Artery

1. What is the title of the diagram?

_____

2. Why do you think these illustrations are called "cross sections"?

_____

3. Judging from the title, are real human arteries larger, smaller, or the same size as the ones shown in the diagram?

_____

4. Which of the arteries above leaves the most room for blood to flow through?

_____

5. Why do you suppose doctors tell their patients to eat foods that are low in fat?

_____

Check your answers on page 68.

Charts _____

Charts can be useful for organizing information. Information in charts is organized in vertical *columns*. Each column has a *heading*. The headings on the chart below are "Activity," "Cal./Min.," and "Cal./Hr."

Directions: Examine the chart carefully and answer the questions using the information in the chart.

Calories Burned During Different Activities		
Activity	**Cal./Min.**	**Cal./Hr.**
Lying down, relaxing	1.5	90
Standing, playing a trumpet	2.1	126
Driving a motorcycle	3.4	204
Weeding a garden	5.0	300
Carrying a 130-lb. load up stairs	30.7	1,842
Cross-country running	10.6	636
Climbing stairs	9.8–13.8	588–828
Picking up around the house	5.9	354
Making beds	5.4	324
Walking across a plowed field	7.6	456
Walking rapidly	5.2	312

Source: *Biological Principles with Human Perspectives* by Gideon Nelson

1. What is the title of the chart?

   _____

2. What information is shown in the second and third columns?

   _____

3. Which activity burns the most calories in an hour?

   _____

4. How many calories do you burn each minute you spend weeding a garden?

   _____

5. Will you burn more calories making beds or picking up around the house?

   _____

6. What burns more calories—walking rapidly for two minutes or cross-country running for one minute?

   _____

Check your answers on pages 68–69.

Chart Practice

Directions: After reading the passage below, answer the questions using the information in the chart.

As a science experiment, Karl decided to find out how long it takes things to fall from his bedroom window. It was a very windy day. He collected items from around the house and weighed each item on a kitchen scale. He then dropped one item at a time out of his window and timed each with a stopwatch. These were his results.

Falling Times of Various Household Objects		
Object	**Weight**	**Falling Time**
Paper airplane	.4 oz.	5 seconds
Plastic bag	.8 oz.	2 seconds
Barbie doll	6 oz.	1.03 seconds
Baseball	12 oz.	1.0 seconds
Piece of metal pipe	22 oz.	1.01 seconds
Basketball	30 oz.	1.01 seconds
Large rock	96 oz.	1.0 seconds

1. According to Karl's measurements, which objects had the fastest falling time?

   _____

2. Which fell faster—the baseball or the pipe? Which weighs more?

   _____

3. Look at the times of the last five items on the list. Does weight seem to make a big difference in how fast they fell?

   _____

4. Which object had the slowest falling time? Why do you think it took so long to hit the ground?

   _____

5. Karl made a hypothesis before he started his experiment. He guessed that the more an object weighed, the faster it would fall. Based on the information in the chart, was his hypothesis correct? Why or why not?

   _____

   _____

Check your answers on page 69.

Line Graphs

Line graphs show trends. Line graphs have two *axes*, or reference lines. The axis that runs from left to right is the *horizontal axis*. The axis that runs up and down is the *vertical axis*. Each axis shows a different set of numbers or measurements. The *graph line* shows increases or decreases by moving up or down between the axes.

Directions: Look over each graph and answer the questions that follow.

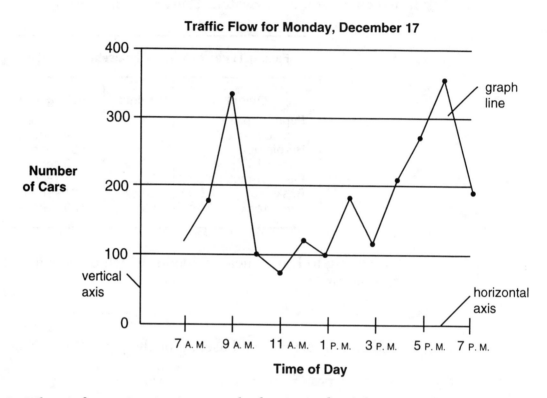

1. What information is given on the horizontal axis?

_____

2. What information is given on the vertical axis?

_____

3. At what two times of day was traffic heaviest?

_____

4. About how many cars were counted at 11:00 A.M? How many were counted at 3:00 P.M.?

_____

5. Based on what you know about street traffic, how would you explain the two high traffic times during the day?

_____

The line graph below is the type produced by a *polygraph*, or lie detector. A polygraph measures changes in the *heart rate*—the number of heartbeats per minute—that often occur when people lie.

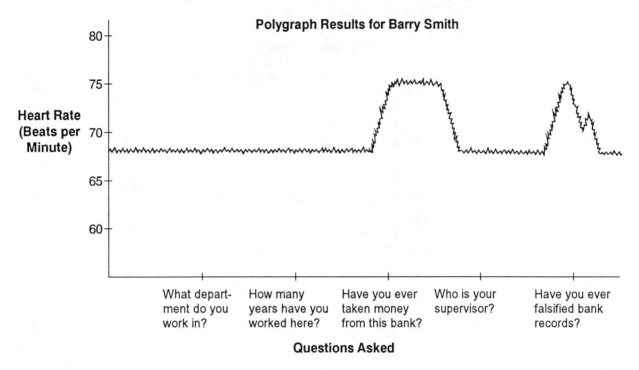

Polygraph Results for Barry Smith

6. What is listed on the vertical axis?

_____

7. What is listed on the horizontal axis?

_____

8. When answering 3 of the 5 questions, Barry's heart rate remains about average for a person sitting at rest. What is that heart rate?

_____

9. What is Barry's heart rate when he is asked if he has taken money from the bank?

_____

10. A person's heart rate usually goes up when he or she gets nervous. One problem with a polygraph test is that people don't always get nervous when they lie. On the other hand, some people get nervous even when they're telling the truth. Based on this information, do these polygraph results tell us for certain whether Barry is lying? If not, what do they tell us?

_____

Check your answers on page 69.

Line Graph Practice

Directions: Read the statements based on the graph below. Write *T* if the statement is true, *F* if it is false.

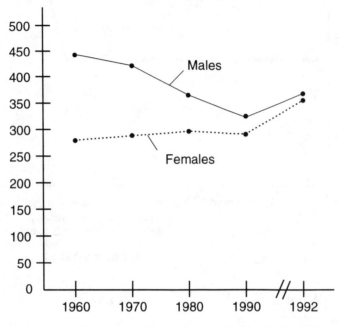

**U. S. Death Rates from Heart Disease,
1960–1986
(per 100,000 population)**

Source: National Center for Health Statistics

_____ **1.** In 1960, about 440 of every 100,000 males died of heart disease.

_____ **2.** In 1980, about 305 of every 100,000 males died of heart disease.

_____ **3.** Between 1960 and 1990, more males than females died of heart disease.

_____ **4.** Between 1960 and 1992, the death rate for heart disease rose for both males and females.

_____ **5.** Between 1960 and 1992, the death rate for heart disease rose and then fell for both males and females.

Check your answers on page 69.

Bar Graphs

The *bar graph* is useful when *comparing* information about different subjects. For example, the bar graph below records the daily sleep requirements for different mammals. By comparing the heights of the bars, you can easily tell which animals need the least and which need the most sleep.

Directions: Answer the questions based on the bar graph alone.

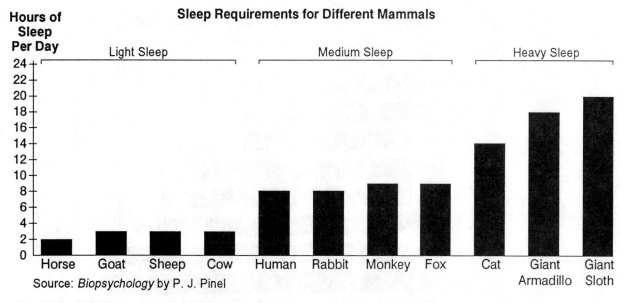

Source: *Biopsychology* by P. J. Pinel

1. According to the graph, which of these mammals is a medium sleeper?

   (1) cow

   (2) giant sloth

   (3) cat

   (4) giant armadillo

   (5) fox

2. From the information on this graph, what general conclusions can you draw about mammals and sleep? Put a check (✔) next to each correct answer.

   _____ **a.** The bigger the mammal, the more sleep it needs.

   _____ **b.** There is a big difference in the amount of sleep different mammals need.

   _____ **c.** Wild animals need more sleep than tame animals.

   _____ **d.** Size does not seem to affect mammals' sleep requirements.

   _____ **e.** Reptiles need less sleep than mammals.

Check your answers on page 69.

Bar Graph Practice _____

A person's *life expectancy* is the number of years he or she can expect to live. As you can see from the graph, the average human life expectancy has changed quite a bit since 700 B.C.

Directions: Study each bar graph and answer the questions that follow.

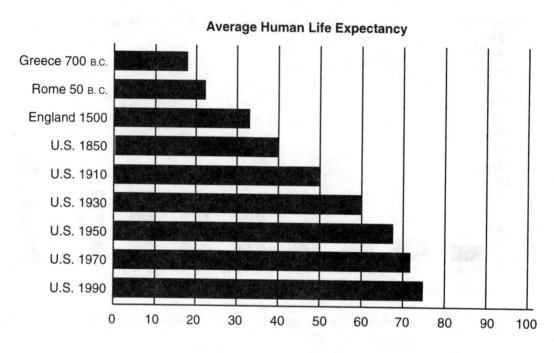

Average Human Life Expectancy

Source: U.S. National Center for Health Statistics

1. In which of the years shown on the graph did human beings have the shortest life expectancy?

   _____

2. In what year could the average U.S. citizen expect to live to age 50?

   _____

3. How much longer did average Americans live in 1990 than in 1910?

   _____

4. What does this graph tell you about human life expectancy over the years?

   _____

5. Can you think of any reasons for the changes in our life expectancy?

   _____

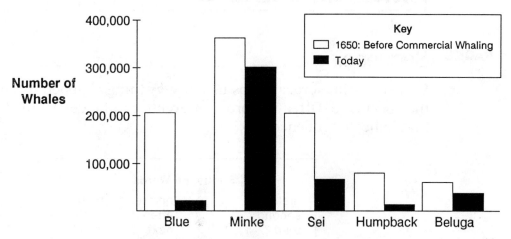

Whale Populations—1650 and Present

Number of Whales

400,000
300,000
200,000
100,000

Blue   Minke   Sei   Humpback   Beluga

Key
☐ 1650: Before Commercial Whaling
■ Today

Source: *Nova: Adventures in Science* by WGBH Educational Foundation

If you look at the upper right-hand corner of this graph, you'll notice a small box called a *key*. This provides information that "unlocks" the meaning of the graph. As you can see, the white bars represent the whale populations *before* people started killing them for profit. The shaded bars represent the whale populations today.

6. Which whale population was largest in 1650?

_____

7. Which whale population is largest today?

_____

8. Which species of whale declined the most in number?

_____

9. What does this graph tell you about the size of whale populations since 1650?

_____

10. What does this graph say about the cause of the decreasing whale populations?

_____

_____

Check your answers on page 70.

ANALYZING IDEAS

TEXT PAGES
96–100

Sequencing

Sequence (time order) helps us tell *why* things happen by showing *when* they occurred. Often the order of events can be determined from words that indicate sequence.

Sequence Words		
first	before	then
second	after	finally
third	next	later
afterward	during	today
in the meantime	since	until

Directions: Underline the sequence words in the sentences and answer the questions.

EXAMPLE

Ines and Berto stopped for ice cream <u>after</u> the movie.

Where did Ines and Berto go first: to the ice cream parlor or to the movie?

to the movie

1. The mechanic checked the spark plugs first; he knew the car wouldn't start if the plugs weren't firing.

   Does the engine start before or after the spark plugs fire?

   _____

2. For years, nuclear power plants have turned out tons of radioactive waste; in the meantime, scientists have searched desperately for a safe way to dispose of the waste.

   According to the statement, were scientists trying to find a safe disposal method before, during, or after the time when nuclear plants produced waste?

   _____

3. After he saw the terrible destruction caused by the atomic bomb, Albert Einstein made many speeches against it.

   Did Einstein make his speeches before or after the first atomic bomb was exploded?

   _____

Check your answers on page 70.

Sequencing Practice

Directions: Read the following passage. Then answer the question that follows.

The Atomic Bomb

The first atomic bomb was exploded in New Mexico on July 16, 1945, in an experiment called the Manhattan Project. The bomb produced an explosion equal to 20,000 tons of dynamite. Within weeks, the U.S. military had dropped two atomic bombs on the Japanese cities of Hiroshima and Nagasaki, helping to end World War II.

Scientists had discovered the atom's basic structure in the early 1900s. However, it was years later when they first understood that vast energy is released when an atom's *nucleus* (center) is split. In the 1930s, scientists split uranium atoms, using a process called *nuclear fission*. Scientists realized that a chain reaction of this nuclear fission would give off incredible amounts of energy. They realized that a designed fission reaction could make a very powerful bomb.

In 1939, scientist Albert Einstein wrote a letter to President Roosevelt telling him about this idea. The federal government provided money to develop the atomic bomb. A plan was approved. The Manhattan Engineer District of the Corps of Engineers began work in Los Alamos, New Mexico, and in 1942 the Manhattan Project was born.

---

1. Put the events in this list in sequence from earliest to latest by numbering them 1 to 5.

   _____ The United States dropped atomic bombs on Japan.

   _____ Albert Einstein wrote a letter to President Roosevelt.

   _____ Scientists first split the atom.

   _____ The first atomic bomb was exploded.

   _____ The Manhattan Project began in Los Alamos, New Mexico.

Check your answers on page 70.

Logical Sequence

When no sequence words are found in a sentence or group of sentences, you must use common sense to determine the time order.

Directions: List the letters of each group of events in their logical order.

EXAMPLE

   a. Charlie bandages his finger.

   b. Charlie cuts his finger.

   Logical order: _b_ , _a_

1. **a.** Galileo views the Milky Way through a telescope.

   b. Galileo builds a telescope.

   Logical order: ____ , ____

2. **a.** The temperature drops below freezing.

   b. Heavy rains fall on all the major roadways.

   c. The highway becomes a sheet of ice.

   Logical order: ____ , ____ , ____

3. **a.** The Wright brothers fly the first airplane.

   b. Pan American Airways announces the first passenger flights across the Atlantic.

   c. Charles Lindbergh makes the first solo nonstop transatlantic flight.

   Logical order: ____ , ____ , ____

4. **a.** Neon gas is put into light bulbs to give the light color.

   b. Thomas Edison invents the light bulb.

   c. Benjamin Franklin discovers electricity.

   d. Hollywood Boulevard glows with neon lights.

   Logical order: ____ , ____ , ____ , ____

5. **a.** The element carbon is identified by scientists.

   b. Engineers create the first artificial diamonds out of carbon.

   c. Factories use artificial diamonds as cutting tools.

   d. Scientists discover that diamonds are made of carbon.

   Logical order: ____ , ____ , ____ , ____

Check your answers on pages 70–71.

Cause and Effect

Things often occur in sequence because something has caused something else to happen. This is called *cause* and *effect*. A *cause* is something that makes another thing happen; the *effect* is the thing that happens.

Directions: Fill in the blanks with the most logical cause or effect.

EXAMPLE

The earth's crust extends about 40 miles beneath the surface of Earth. Strong pushing and pulling movements deep within the earth's crust can be felt above the surface as earthquakes.

Cause: *movements within the earth's crust*

Effect: *earthquakes*

1. Huge sea waves called *tsunamis* result when strong movements within the earth's crust occur beneath an ocean floor.

   Cause: _____

   Effect: _____

2. In 1906, California's San Andreas Fault shifted. Shaking was felt across the state, but damage was greatest in San Francisco.

   Cause: _____

   Effect: _____

3. A *seismograph* records ground movements in an earthquake. The pen or light ray on a seismograph makes a wavy line whenever the ground moves.

   Cause: _____

   Effect: _____

4. Before an earthquake, well water often becomes muddy, the ground above a fault line moves, and animals behave in unusual ways. Because they know to watch for these signs, scientists may learn to predict earthquakes.

   Cause: _____

   Effect: _____

Check your answers on page 71.

Cause and Effect Practice

Directions: Read the passage carefully. Then answer the questions that follow.

Scientists call it *polytetrafluoroethylene* (poly•tetra•fluoro•ethylene). The DuPont Company calls it a winner. The rest of us know it as *Teflon*, the slippery, nonstick material used in thousands of products from frying pans to artificial heart valves and space suits. It is also one of the many scientific discoveries made completely by accident.

In 1938, while working on a project, a DuPont chemist named Roy Plunkett opened the valve on a tank of tetrafluoroethylene gas. To his surprise, nothing came out. The tank was heavy, so he knew it was full of something. He cut open the tank. What he found inside was unlike anything he had ever seen. The molecules of the gas had *polymerized*—the light molecules of the gas had combined with each other to form heavier molecules. The result was a white, waxy material that was also amazingly slippery. Plunkett and his co-workers soon found a way to create the new polymer, but they had no idea what to do with it. Plunkett's discovery was set aside.

A few months later, a group of scientists came to DuPont. They were working on the first atomic bomb and were having problems with some of their gaskets. The gaskets, they said, would dissolve every time they were exposed to uranium gas, which was needed to produce a nuclear chain reaction. Did DuPont have a better gasket material?

The DuPont engineers immediately began testing the new polymer. They soon discovered that besides being slippery, the new material was also very durable. They began using it to make gaskets and valves for the atomic bomb. They produced Teflon parts for the U.S. Defense Department during the rest of World War II.

After the war was over, engineers began experimenting with commercial uses for Teflon. The first Teflon pans were introduced to the public in 1960, but they were a bit disappointing. Although Teflon was the perfect nonstick surface for cooking, engineers had a difficult time making it stick to the surface of the pans. After years of testing and research, however, they found a way to make it work. Teflon was also used in many other products and has become one of DuPont's most successful products. It is also one of the most profitable accidents Roy Plunkett ever had.

1. From the information supplied in the passage, what caused the tetrafluoroethylene gas to form into a solid?

_____

2. What effect did uranium gas have on the original gaskets?

_____

3. What effect did the gas have on the Teflon gaskets?

_____

4. Number the events in the order in which they occurred.

_____ Plunkett discovered a strange material inside a tank.

_____ Tetrafluoroethylene gas polymerized in a DuPont laboratory.

_____ Scientists developed a way to produce Teflon.

_____ Teflon frying pans were introduced on the market.

_____ The atomic bomb was invented.

5. Based on the information in the passage, which of the following was *not* an effect of Plunkett's discovery?

   (1) Scientists found a way to build the atomic bomb.

   (2) Consumers had a new type of cookware.

   (3) Artificial heart valves were improved.

   (4) The DuPont company made more money.

   (5) The tetrafluoroethylene gas polymerized inside its tank.

6. Which title best describes the main idea of the passage?

   (1) Teflon: Our Friend in Wartime and Peace

   (2) The Remarkable Story of Teflon

   (3) Roy Plunkett: Portrait of a Genius

   (4) The Many Different Uses of Teflon

   (5) Great Accidental Discoveries in Science

Check your answers on page 71.

Inferences

Sometimes writers don't directly tell you everything they mean. Instead, they *imply* (hint at) some things by the way they write. When writers imply something, you must *infer* (figure out) what they mean. This skill is called *making inferences*.

Directions: After each statement, write the inference that can be made.

EXAMPLE

Katya stopped smoking when she learned she was pregnant.

What inference can you make about smoking?

that smoking is bad for pregnant women

1. The man who reported the UFO had just spent five hours in a bar.

   What inference can you make about the UFO sighting?

   _____

2. In terms of power, speed, and versatility, the new generation of home computers is the most advanced ever. Better still—you don't have to be a rocket scientist to use one!

   What four things about *previous* generations of home computers can you infer?

   a. _____

   b. _____

   c. _____

   d. _____

3. With the price of silver at an all-time low, it is now cheaper than ever to produce photographic film.

   What inference can you make about the production of photographic film?

   _____

4. Controlling the weather would be good for our planet. No matter what the experts say, this could only help our environment.

   What can you infer about the experts' opinion about weather control?

   _____

Check your answers on page 71.

Inference Practice

Directions: Read each passage and answer the questions that follow.

Micromotors: Motors of the Future?

Imagine electric motors smaller than the width of a human hair. They do exist. And if scientists are correct, these *micromotors* could prove as important to society as computers are.

Micromotors are fully functional electric motors that are built on very small scales. Some have gears with cogs the size of human blood cells. Their springs and cranks often are so small they can be inhaled accidentally. And while scientists are still not sure how these motors might be used, some of their suggestions seem more like science fiction than science.

---

1. What can you infer about the scientists' suggestions?

_____

For instance, some say micromotors could power tiny buzzsaws to be used in delicate microsurgery. Swarms of insect-sized robots might one day clean office buildings faster and more cheaply than humans do. Microscopic machines might be injected into the bloodstream to scrape the fatty deposits from the walls of arteries. "Smart pills" might be developed to dispense an exact amount of medication through tiny valves.

---

2. What can you infer about the pills that are used today?

_____

Most seem to agree that these uses are years away. Some of the proposed uses may be impossible. But scientists point to the now much-used microchip and suggest similarities. In these early days of the micromotor, no one can predict what uses it could have.

---

3. What can you infer about the early days of microchips?

_____

Check your answers on page 71.

BUILDING VOCABULARY

TEXT PAGES
129–130 Compound Words _____

Compound words are made by putting two words together. For example, the words *basket* and *ball*, when put together, make the word *basketball.*

Directions: Use the words in the box below to form a compound word for each definition.

power	fly	load	water	under
boat	house	dose	trap	light
horse	over	span	man	hole
candle	wing	coat	work	step

EXAMPLE

a fly that is commonly found in the house:

housefly

1. work done around the house:

_____

2. a dose of medicine that is more than the prescribed amount:

_____

3. the combined length, or *span*, of the wings of an airplane or a bird:

_____

4. a place where boats are kept:

_____

5. beneath the surface of an ocean or a lake:

_____

6. Using the list of words above, try to form at least five new compound words. Write the words below.

_____

Check your answers on page 72.

Defining Compound Words

Directions: In the following paragraph, the compound words are set in *italics*. Read the paragraph and write your own definitions for the compound words on the spaces below.

It seems ***everywhere*** we turn, another ***headline*** tells us about the ***overflow*** of garbage. These warnings are ***commonplace***. However, the solutions are more difficult to find. There are several ways to dispose of garbage, but each has its ***drawbacks***. ***Landfills*** are the most ***widespread*** method of handling waste. Unfortunately, these fill up quickly, and it is difficult to find new dump sites. The public ***outcry*** against them is strong. Landfills are ***eyesores***, and the smell can be ***overpowering***. Some communities burn their waste, but this method pollutes the air. Most experts agree that recycling is the most ***worthwhile*** approach to waste management. Despite many ***setbacks***, the recycling movement is gaining strength.

EXAMPLE everywhere *in every place*

1. headline _____

2. overflow _____

3. commonplace _____

4. drawback _____

5. landfill _____

6. widespread _____

7. outcry _____

8. eyesore _____

9. overpowering _____

10. worthwhile _____

11. setback _____

Check your answers on page 72.

Word Parts

Many scientific words are made up of several word parts put together. The main part of the word is called the *root* of the word. An addition to the beginning of a word is called a *prefix*. An addition to the end of a word is called a *suffix*. Look at these examples:

de- (prefix) + compose (root) = decompose

fix (root) + -able (suffix) = fixable

Directions: By combining word parts, you can form new words with new meanings. In the exercise below, a prefix is defined and followed by either a root or a suffix. Add the prefix to the other word parts to form two new words. Write the definitions on the lines provided.

EXAMPLE

tele- (far away)

a. scope (an instrument for seeing) <u>telescope</u>

Definition: <u>an instrument for seeing things that are far away</u>

b. phone (an instrument for hearing) <u>telephone</u>

Definition: <u>an instrument for hearing things that are far away</u>

1. bi- (two)

a. cycle (something with wheels) _____

Definition: _____

b. -ped (something with feet) _____

Definition: _____

2. pre- (before)

a. historic (having to do with written history) _____

Definition: _____

b. natal (birth) _____

Definition: _____

3. ex- (out)

a. hale (to breathe) _____

Definition: _____

b. tract (to pull) _____

Definition: _____

4. astro- (having to do with outer space)

    a. naut (a sailor or traveler) _____

    Definition: _____

    b. biology (the study of living things) _____

    Definition: _____

5. inter- (between or among)

    a. national (having to do with nations) _____

    Definition: _____

    b. stellar (having to do with the stars) _____

    Definition: _____

6. herbi- (having to do with plants)

    a. -cide (killing or something that kills) _____

    Definition: _____

    b. vorous (feeding on) _____

    Definition: _____

7. rhino- (having to do with the nose)

    a. -ceros (horn) _____

    Definition: _____

    b. -plasty (plastic surgery) _____

    Definition: _____

8. uni- (one)

    a. lingual (language) _____

    Definition: _____

    b. son (sound) _____

    Definition: _____

Check your answers on page 72.

Context Clues

Often the meaning of a word can be guessed by looking at the *context*, the information surrounding the word in the sentence or passage. You might read, for instance, that a nuclear war would be *catastrophic*. From the context, you can guess that *catastrophic* probably means *very bad*.

Directions: Circle the definition that best fits the word in italics, using context as your only clue.

1. With their current *capacity* of 500 gallons, the new storage tanks will hold twice as much gasoline as the old ones.

   (1) lifespan

   (2) cost

   (3) weight resistance

   (4) ability to hold liquid or other substances

2. Scientists had to track the two tornadoes *concurrently* because they both occurred on the same day.

   (1) secretly

   (2) quickly

   (3) at the same time

   (4) bravely

3. When natural gas was used for indoor lighting, explosions were common. One of the benefits of electricity is that it is not as *volatile* as natural gas.

   (1) inconvenient

   (2) uncommon

   (3) explosive

   (4) expensive

4. Once we realized how far off our measurements were, we began to question the *fidelity* of our measuring instruments.

   (1) accuracy

   (2) durability

   (3) wisdom

   (4) security

Check your answers on page 72.

Context Clues Practice _____

Directions: Read the following passage carefully. Use the context to help you define the numbered words. Write the definitions on the numbered lines at the bottom of the page.

Even as Halley's comet passed the earth in 1910, scientists were already preparing for its next visit. They would have a long wait. Since Halley's comet has a **period**[1] of 76 years, they knew it would not pass again until 1986. But when its **luminous**[2] tail finally lit up the sky, scientists were ready. **Astronomers**[3] around the world stood by with telescopes and radio equipment, ready to observe this **astral**[4] traveler.

Their **diligence**[5] paid off. In 1986, scientists made one of their most important discoveries about Halley's comet. They found **conclusive**[6] proof that it did not come from our solar system. Using a **sophisticated**[7] new method of analyzing chemicals, scientists discovered a strange combination of **carbon 12 and carbon 13**[8] in the comet's tail. They had never seen this combination on earth or on any of the meteors or planets ever observed. This startling chemical evidence taught scientists that Halley's comet must have **originated**[9] in a system of planets very far from and very different from our own.

---

1. _____

2. _____

3. _____

4. _____

5. _____

6. _____

7. _____

8. _____

9. _____

Check your answers on pages 72–73.

Scientific Language _____

Scientific language often seems difficult. By reading it phrase by phrase, however, and looking for word and context clues, it can be translated into simpler language.

Directions: Read the sentences and rewrite them using simple, everyday words. Try to use word parts and context clues to figure out the words you don't understand. Use a dictionary if these clues don't help.

EXAMPLE

Overconsumption of coffee can lead to symptoms of nervous anxiety.

Drinking too much coffee can make you jittery.

1. The absence of rain, coupled with unusually high temperatures, resulted in widespread crop failure.

2. Few people would deny that modern automobiles are superior in terms of speed and maneuverability to those manufactured 20 years ago.

3. By observing and recording abnormalities in the orbits of the other planets, scientists deduced the existence of Pluto without actually seeing it.

4. Anyone proposing the further deforestation of the Amazon rain forests should consider its impact on the rich variety of species in the region.

5. Exposure to the cigarette fumes exhaled by nearby smokers can prove to be harmful to one's health.

Check your answers on page 73.

Scientific Language Practice

Directions: Read the following passage. As you read, translate the sentences in *italics* into everyday language. Rewrite them in your own words on the lines provided.

EXAMPLE

Anyone who has ever grown tired of wearing corrective lenses should consider radial keratotomy. This revolutionary new type of surgery can correct bad eyesight. It is more affordable than most types of surgery. *It can be performed in approximately twenty minutes, with a minimum of discomfort.* And the patient can return to work after only a few days.

Anyone who doesn't like wearing glasses or contacts should think about radial keratotomy.

1. _____
_____
_____
_____

Radial keratotomy can, in rare instances, result in the further impairment of vision. For this reason, many eye doctors do not recommend this surgery. These doctors also point out that the surgery may make eyes even worse as a patient gets older. *Other doctors, though, consider these risks to be minimal. These doctors believe that the benefits of radial keratotomy outweigh any risks associated with this type of surgery.*

2. _____
_____
_____
_____

3. _____
_____
_____
_____
_____
_____

Check your answers on page 73.

EVALUATING IDEAS

TEXT PAGES
161–163 ## Values and Beliefs

Values are the things we think are important. They help us make decisions about life. Whenever we consider whether an idea is good or bad, we judge it according to our values, the things we think are most important.

Directions: After reading the following statements, put a check (✔) next to the value that you think is *most important* to the person making the statement.

EXAMPLE

We should protect our forest lands from economic development.

____ economic development   ✔ environmental protection

It is clear that the speaker values environmental protection more than economic development.

1. We should spend more money on feeding people and less on exploring outer space.

   ____ social welfare   ____ scientific knowledge

2. Scientists should not conduct painful experiments on animals, even if those experiments could save human lives.

   ____ medical research   ____ animal welfare

3. Businesses that manufacture toxic chemicals should pay to have them removed from the environment.

   ____ economic development   ____ environmental protection

4. People should conserve our nation's fuel supplies by driving more slowly.

   ____ energy conservation   ____ time saving

5. Since the world already has too many people, nobody should be allowed to have more than two children.

   ____ population control   ____ individual liberties

6. The United States should spend more on research to invent new, money-making technologies.

   ____ research and development   ____ saving money now

Check your answers on page 73.

Values and Beliefs Practice

Directions: Read the following fictional article. For each value listed below, decide whether people who hold that value would be *for* or *against* Longevitol. Put a check (✔) next to the correct answer.

Miracle Drug Discovered!

Scientists have announced the discovery of an amazing new drug. The drug, Longevitol, reverses the process of aging. Scientists say it restores the bodies of old people, making them young and healthy. It can keep people alive for hundreds, even thousands of years. It can help government leaders to live for centuries, making them wiser.

Longevitol is made from the glands of male sea turtles. Since a single sea turtle can produce only a tiny amount of the drug, thousands of sea turtles will have to be raised in captivity so their glands can be surgically removed.

Unfortunately, Longevitol is very expensive. The drug must be taken every day to keep the body young. With the high cost of producing the drug and the heavy dosages required, scientists predict that only very wealthy people will be able to afford it.

---

1. Value: Growing old is the worst thing that can happen to a person.

   ____ for Longevitol   ____ against Longevitol

2. Value: Scientists should spend their time developing drugs that combat AIDS and cancer, not the human condition of aging.

   ____ for Longevitol   ____ against Longevitol

3. Value: Animals should never be raised for slaughter.

   ____ for Longevitol   ____ against Longevitol

4. Value: Anything that improves government is good for society.

   ____ for Longevitol   ____ against Longevitol

5. Value: Old people should step aside and leave our world's resources for the next generation.

   ____ for Longevitol   ____ against Longevitol

6. Value: Good looks are the most important thing in a person's life.

   ____ for Longevitol   ____ against Longevitol

Check your answers on page 73.

Incomplete Information _____

Values help us make decisions according to what we think is right. *Information* also helps us make decisions. It helps us understand all the facts so we can make informed decisions. However, we don't always get *complete information* about issues. Sometimes we get only a part of the information we need to make decisions.

In each of the following exercises, the author is trying to convince you to do something. You will find that each passage includes only part of the information you need to make a decision.

Directions: Read each passage and put a check (✔) by the questions you would ask in order to have complete information.

> Every home owner should buy a new, fuel-efficient water heater. The old water heaters burn too much gas and cost too much to operate. With a new water heater, you'll burn less gas and save money.

1. What other information would help you decide whether to buy a new water heater?

   _____ **a.** How much hot water does the average family use?

   _____ **b.** How much will a new water heater cost?

   _____ **c.** How much money will I save with a new water heater?

   _____ **d.** Is gas less expensive in other parts of the country?

   _____ **e.** Is it safe to wash all my laundry in hot water?

> Hundreds of people die in airplane crashes each year. The government should pass strict new laws to keep airlines from letting their planes get old and outdated.

2. What other information would help you decide whether the government should pass new regulations?

   _____ **a.** How many airplanes are there in the United States?

   _____ **b.** Do airlines charge their customers too much?

   _____ **c.** Are most crashes caused by old and outdated airplanes?

   _____ **d.** What is the average age of planes that crash?

   _____ **e.** How many people survive airplane crashes?

Vote for a longer school day. In Japan, the school days are longer and students score much higher on tests than U.S. students do.

3. What other information would help you decide whether to vote for a longer school day?

_____ **a.** Do the Japanese use the same tests as Americans?

_____ **b.** Do the Japanese students like the longer school days?

_____ **c.** Do Japanese students get higher-paying jobs when they get out of school?

_____ **d.** How many Japanese students are there in the United States?

_____ **e.** Do Japanese students spend more total hours in school than American students?

Philsley High School needs new computers. There is a new type of computer program that teaches math and science better than any of the old programs. With new computers, these remarkable new programs could be run on beautiful, full-color computer screens.

4. What other information would help you decide whether to buy new computers?

_____ **a.** Can the school afford new computers?

_____ **b.** Will the old computers run the new programs?

_____ **c.** Are students more interested in shop classes than in math and science classes?

_____ **d.** Why weren't the new programs available last year?

_____ **e.** Will the students learn better on full-color computer screens?

Check your answers on page 73.

Bias

Not all the information we hear or read can be accepted as fact. Information sometimes comes from a source that is *biased* (prejudiced) toward one side of an issue. For example, you might want to know whether riding a bicycle is better exercise than jogging. A sporting-goods salesperson would be likely to answer yes because he or she wants to sell you a bicycle. Although the salesperson is not necessarily lying, we have reasons to question his or her opinion. The salesperson is *biased*.

Directions: After each question below there are two sources of information. Write a *Y* in front of the source that is biased toward a "yes" answer. Write an *N* in front of the source that is biased toward a "no" answer.

1. Will a new energy-efficient gas heater save me enough money to pay for itself?

    _____ **a.** brochures from a manufacturer of energy-efficient gas heaters

    _____ **b.** a person who sells electric heaters

2. Do Japanese cars get better gas mileage than American cars?

    _____ **a.** a Chevrolet salesperson

    _____ **b.** the Japanese trade representative to the United States

3. Will a landfill in my neighborhood be bad for my family's health?

    _____ **a.** a home owner next to the suggested landfill location

    _____ **b.** the president of a waste-disposal company

4. Is red meat an important part of a healthy diet?

    _____ **a.** a butcher

    _____ **b.** a vegetarian

5. Do American children watch too much TV?

    _____ **a.** the producer of children's cartoon shows

    _____ **b.** a book publisher

6. Is nuclear power a safe way to make electricity?

    _____ **a.** a nuclear power plant spokesperson

    _____ **b.** an environmental activist

Check your answers on pages 73–74.

Reliable Sources

While some people may be *unbiased* sources of information, they may not know enough to be *reliable sources*. A dentist, for example, probably would not be a reliable source for information on tree diseases. A police officer, on the other hand, might be a very reliable source for information on protecting your home from burglars.

Directions: For each question, select the most reliable source of information from the list below.

local garden club	home builder	TV repairperson
family doctor	plumber	fire fighter
executive secretary	local school board	mechanic

1. Which schools offer help for children with learning disabilities?

   _____

2. How often do I need to change the oil in my car?

   _____

3. Why do my roses keep dying?

   _____

4. Can my television be fixed?

   _____

5. What is the correct format for a business letter?

   _____

6. What equipment do I need to unclog a drain?

   _____

7. Is my bedroom floor strong enough to support a waterbed?

   _____

8. Where should I install smoke detectors in my home?

   _____

Check your answers on page 74.

POST-TEST

The Post-Test should give you a good idea of how well you have learned the skills you have practiced in this book. You should take the Post-Test after you have completed all the exercises.

Directions: Study each passage or illustration, then answer the questions that follow.

Questions 1–3 are based on the following passage.

The Balance of Predators and Prey

Before 1907, there were about 4,000 deer and a large population of mountain lions and wolves on the Grand Canyon's Kaibab Plateau. The government felt that deer had much more value in nature than did mountain lions and wolves. Beginning in 1907, the mountain lions and wolves were either killed or relocated. By 1925, the deer population had grown to 100,000.

Unfortunately, the Kaibab Plateau could not produce nearly enough food to feed such a large herd. Soon the deer had eaten all the grass, bushes, and small trees on the range. The Kaibab Plateau looked like a huge, overgrazed pasture. In less than two years, 40 percent of the herd starved to death. The deer continued to die until only 10,000 were left. With fewer deer grazing on the plateau, the plant life slowly began to grow back. To this day, however, the damage can still be seen. The Kaibab Plateau is a forceful reminder of the delicate balance between predators and prey.

---

1. What is the main idea of this passage?

   (1) Mountain lions and wolves are the natural enemies of deer.

   (2) The government can be very successful in raising large herds of deer.

   (3) The Kaibab Plateau was almost destroyed by deer.

   (4) It is deer, not wolves, that pose the greatest threat to the Grand Canyon.

   (5) Interfering with natural systems can lead to disaster.

2. Which of these statements expresses an opinion?

   (1) The deer ate all the bushes, grass, and small trees.

   (2) By 1925, the deer population on the Kaibab Plateau had grown to 100,000.

   (3) Deer have much more value in nature than do mountain lions and wolves.

   (4) In less than two years, 40 percent of the deer starved to death.

   (5) The Kaibab Plateau could not produce nearly enough food to feed such a large herd.

3. What effect did removing the predators have on the Kaibab Plateau?

   (1) The government started a program to increase the deer population.

   (2) The deer population grew to about 100,000.

   (3) The Kaibab Plateau could not produce enough food to feed the deer.

   (4) The deer devoured all the grass, trees, and bushes.

   (5) The deer starved to death.

Questions 4–5 are based on the following passage.

Clues to Early Man

In the 1920s and 1930s, scientists discovered a large group of fossils in a cave in northern China. The fossils, at least 300,000 years old, showed the remains of small, ape-like people who many believe to be early ancestors of modern humans. Scientists named these people *Homo erectus*. Their ancient remains have given scientists many clues to how modern man may have developed.

Scientists used the clues to develop hypotheses about the *Homo erectus* people. For example, the bones found showed that they stood about five feet tall and probably walked on two feet. The remains of charred animal bones in the cave meant that *Homo erectus* knew how to cook meat over a fire. Stone chopping tools, also found in the caves, showed that *Homo erectus* had the mental scope as well as the highly developed hands and thumbs needed to create and use tools.

---

4. From the evidence found in the cave, what hypotheses can you make about *Homo erectus*? Put a check (✔) next to each correct hypothesis.

    _____ **a.** They ate only plants.

    _____ **b.** They knew how to hunt.

    _____ **c.** They lived in trees.

    _____ **d.** They lived in groups.

    _____ **e.** They lived billions of years ago.

5. Which step in the scientific method is explained in the second paragraph?

    (1) Scientists asked questions about *Homo erectus*.

    (2) Scientists gathered the facts about *Homo erectus*.

    (3) Scientists used the facts to make hypotheses.

    (4) Scientists tested their hypotheses.

    (5) Scientists prepared a theory.

Questions 6–7 are based on the following passage.

Keeping the Air Clean

Studies by the National Aeronautics and Space Administration (NASA) show that growing plants indoors can actually help clean up the air.

NASA scientists had hoped to use plants to create oxygen in spaceships. They experimented with plants and *photosynthesis*. Photosynthesis is a process in which plants make their own food while also releasing oxygen. This process renews the earth's oxygen supply.

During the experiment, scientists found that plants not only produce oxygen but also seem to absorb harmful gases. Benzene, carbon monoxide, and nitrous oxide—all commonly found in modern buildings—seem to disappear when plants are nearby. While plants cannot remove dust or cigarette smoke from a room, scientists believe they can help clean up the air in stuffy, enclosed places.

---

6. What does the passage imply about dust in the air?

   (1) Plants don't remove dust from the air.

   (2) Dust is common on space shuttles.

   (3) Dust is harmful to people.

   (4) Modern buildings do not contain dust.

   (5) Dust can be absorbed by plants during photosynthesis.

7. *"How many plants does it take to make enough oxygen for one human?"* To answer this question, what would you need to know? Put a check (✔) next to each correct answer.

   _____ **a.** Do plants produce benzene?

   _____ **b.** How much oxygen does one plant produce?

   _____ **c.** Is there any dust in space?

   _____ **d.** Does the human smoke cigarettes?

   _____ **e.** How much oxygen do humans need?

Questions 8-9 are based on the following chart and passage.

Thermal Conductivity of Different Materials	
Material	**Thermal Conductivity W/m · K**
Good Conductors	
Silver	418
Copper	400
Aluminum	238
Iron	82
Average Conductors	
Ice	2.2
Concrete	0.8
Floor tile	0.7
Water	0.6
Glass	0.4
Poor Conductors (good insulators)	
Wood	0.2
Snow	0.16
Fiberboard	0.1
Cotton	0.08
Glass wool	0.04
Styrofoam	0.033
Air	0.024
Vacuum	0

Source: *Principles of Physics* by Frank J. Blatt

A *thermal conductor* is any material that carries—or conducts—heat or cold. Good thermal conductors allow heat and cold to pass through them. They heat up and cool down quickly. The higher a material's thermal conductivity, the better heat energy passes through it.

Insulators are materials that do not conduct heat or cold well. They are used in buildings to keep heat or cold from passing through them. The lower a material's thermal conductivity, the better it insulates.

8. Which of these materials conduct heat better than concrete? Put a check (✔) next to each correct answer.

_____ **a.** floor tile

_____ **b.** iron

_____ **c.** fiberboard

_____ **d.** copper

_____ **e.** air

9. Which of these would make the best insulation for a house?

(1) concrete

(2) wood

(3) glass

(4) Styrofoam

(5) aluminum

Questions 10–13 are based on the following passage.

What Is a Computer Virus?

Computer viruses are programs created by people to attack and destroy computer information. New types of viruses such as logic bombs and worms are being developed constantly. Computer viruses have caused millions of dollars in damage to university, corporate, and government computer systems. Most are spread from one computer to another through shared *software*—computer programs stored on a small disk. Some are so contagious they can be spread through the telephone wires when computers are hooked up to them.

Like human viruses, computer viruses spread very quickly once they enter a system. A virus is programmed by its creator to invade and infect certain kinds of information. The infection usually happens in three steps. First, the virus instructs the computer to tell it what kind of information is available to attack. For example, a virus can attack software, documents, or almost any other kind of stored information. After identifying the stored information it wants to attack, the virus copies itself onto that target. Finally, the virus attacks the target by making millions of copies of itself. It creates so much new data that the target information is damaged or erased. And viruses can be very hard to cure. An infected computer may stay down (out of service) for days or even weeks with its "illness."

So far, nobody has found a foolproof way to protect against viral infections. Luckily, programs that detect and destroy some viruses are available. But as long as people keep inventing new viruses, no computer system is completely safe from this form of electronic disease.

---

10. From the context of the second paragraph, how would you define the word *software*?

(1) a type of stored information

(2) a part of a computer's hardware

(3) something that destroys information

(4) foam padding to protect the computer from damage

(5) something that reproduces and spreads quickly

11. What does the second paragraph imply about human viruses?

   (1) They can be spread to computers.

   (2) They can spread over the phone lines.

   (3) They have caused considerable damage to universities in the United States.

   (4) They do not affect computer hardware.

   (5) They spread quickly.

12. The author of this passage would probably agree that

   (1) computer viruses don't really pose much of a problem

   (2) human viruses and computer viruses are almost identical

   (3) computer viruses can be very helpful

   (4) computer viruses are destructive and unnecessary

   (5) it is easy to protect computers from viruses

13. Number the steps of the computer virus infection in their logical sequence.

   _____ Select and infect target programs.

   _____ Make many copies on target programs.

   _____ Find out from the computer about its different types of stored information.

Questions 14–16 are based on the following graph.

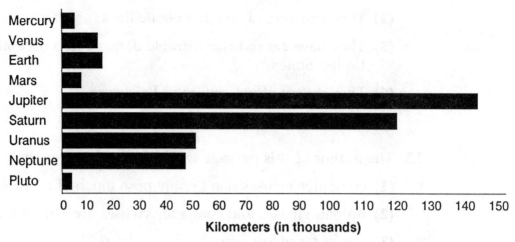

The *diameter* of a planet is the distance from one side to the other, going through the center. The graph above shows the diameters of the planets in our solar system.

14. Which is the largest planet shown on the graph?

(1) Uranus

(2) Earth

(3) Neptune

(4) Jupiter

(5) Saturn

15. What is the approximate diameter of the planet Uranus?

(1) 50 kilometers

(2) 52 kilometers

(3) 500 kilometers

(4) 5,000 kilometers

(5) 50,000 kilometers

16. Gravity is stronger on Jupiter than it is on any of the other planets. This is probably because gravity has something to do with the

(1) size of a planet

(2) distance of a planet from the sun

(3) shape of a planet

(4) name of a planet

(5) temperature of a planet

Questions 17–18 are based on the following passage.

Carbon Dating

How do scientists know how old a plant or animal fossil is? They use a technique called *carbon dating*. Carbon dating helps scientists find the age of a dead plant or animal by looking at how much *radiocarbon* it contains.

Radiocarbon is produced whenever sunlight combines with nitrogen in the atmosphere. It is in the air we breathe, the water we drink, and the plants and animals we eat. Every living thing consumes radiocarbon.

Once a living thing stops living, it stops consuming. The amount of radiocarbon inside the plant or animal steadily decreases as the plant or animal decays. But although an animal's body might stop decaying after a few years, the radiocarbon inside it does not. It decays very slowly. In fact, radiocarbon will still show signs of decay 50,000 years after its host has died.

To find out how old a fossil is, scientists simply measure its remaining radiocarbon. This measurement tells scientists approximately how long the plant or animal has been dead. They can closely guess the age of anything that died within the last 50,000 years.

17. According to the passage, which of these statements is true?

    (1) Radiocarbon causes all living things to die.

    (2) A lack of radiocarbon causes animals to die.

    (3) Animals stop consuming radiocarbon when they die.

    (4) Radiocarbon causes animals to grow older.

    (5) Plants and animals cause radiocarbon to be created.

18. What hypothesis would you make if you found an animal fossil and all the radiocarbon had decayed?

    (1) The animal has been dead for more than 50,000 years.

    (2) The animal has been dead for a few weeks.

    (3) The animal lived before radiocarbons were created.

    (4) The animal lived in the dark.

    (5) The animal did not breathe or eat.

Questions 19–20 are based on the following graph.

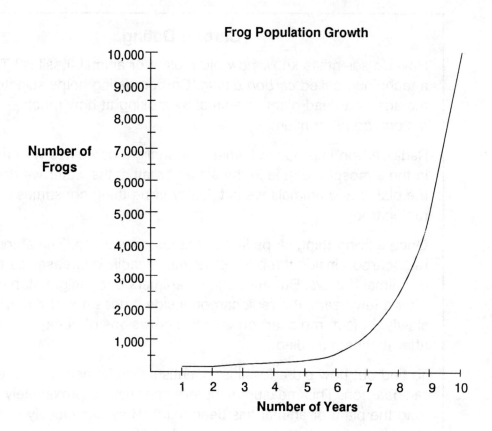

Frog Population Growth

Number of Frogs (y-axis: 1,000 to 10,000)

Number of Years (x-axis: 1 to 10)

One day, Jeremy released 10 bullfrogs in a pond near his house. They were the only bullfrogs in the pond. But as the years went by, the population grew. Jeremy found that the number of bullfrogs doubled every year. He counted 20 frogs after the first year, 40 frogs after the second year, and 80 frogs after the third year. Jeremy kept track of his findings on this line graph.

19. How many frogs were in the pond after 9 years?

    (1) 500

    (2) 1,000

    (3) 2,000

    (4) 3,000

    (5) more than 5,000

20. The graph shows that the frog population

    (1) grew by about 100 frogs per year

    (2) grew slowly every year

    (3) grew slowly at first, and then grew quickly

    (4) did not grow at all

    (5) grew to a certain point and then stopped growing

Questions 21–23 are based on the following passage.

Can Pollution Be a Good Thing?

Since the early 1970's, scientists have warned that pollution is eating away at the ozone layer. This is a problem, they say, because the layer of ozone in our gaseous atmosphere shields us from the sun's most harmful rays. Without ozone, ultraviolet radiation would flood the earth. It would cause severe sunburn, eye damage, and skin cancer in humans. But even though scientists have seen the holes in the ozone layer, they still have not found any increase in ultraviolet radiation.

What could be shielding us from the sun's deadly rays? Scientists believe it could be the pollution itself. Smog might be blocking out ultraviolet radiation at the same time it is eating away the ozone layer. If this is true, we may be facing a classic case of good news and bad news: The good news is we're safe from ultraviolet rays. The bad news is that harmful pollution is what protects us.

---

21. This passage mainly states that

   (1) the ozone layer is disappearing

   (2) ultraviolet radiation is bad for humans

   (3) pollution is not harmful to man

   (4) pollution may be solving one of the problems it creates

   (5) ozone shields us from ultraviolet rays

22. Which of these would be the *most* reliable source of information about the ozone layer?

   (1) a professor of environmental science

   (2) a 1970 investigative report on the ozone

   (3) a United States senator

   (4) a factory owner

   (5) a television talk-show host

23. From the context of the passage, we know that *ozone* is probably

   (1) a type of pollution

   (2) a type of radiation

   (3) a type of gas

   (4) a type of food

   (5) a type of liquid

Questions 24–25 are based on the passage below.

Miracle or Chemical?

Each year, thousands of people come to Naples, Italy, to witness a miracle. They gather in a church and watch while religious leaders turn a small glass vial upside down several times. Suddenly, the material in the vial—believed to be the blood of Saint Januarius—turns from a solid gel into a red liquid.

For decades, scientists have tried to explain this remarkable event. Some believe that the heat from the priest's hand causes the gel to melt. Others believe that the saint's "blood" is not blood at all. They claim that a mixture of water, salt, and *molysite*—a mineral that was available six centuries ago—forms a dark gel that not only looks like blood but also turns to liquid when it is touched or tilted. This special type of chemical reaction is called *thixotropy*.

Despite their continued interest, researchers will likely never get a chance to test their theory. The Catholic church does not allow the vial to be opened.

[adapted from *Health* magazine, Feb./Mar. 1992]

24. The people who believe in the miracle of Saint Januarius would probably agree that

    (1) the vial contains water, salt, and molysite

    (2) heat from candles causes the gel to melt

    (3) most miracles are fakes

    (4) scientists are almost always right

    (5) there are some things that science can never explain

25. Which one of the following people would most likely be biased in favor of a scientific explanation?

    (1) a priest

    (2) a nun

    (3) a tourist

    (4) a chemist

    (5) a TV talk-show host

POST-TEST EVALUATION CHART

Use the answer key on page 65 to check your Post-Test answers. Find the number of each question you missed on this chart and circle it in the third column. Then you will know which chapters you might need to review before you move on to Contemporary's *GED Test 3: Science* book.

Chapter	Skill	Item Numbers	Number Correct
The Scientific Method	Fact/Opinion Hypothesis Scientific Method	2 4, 16, 18 5	____/5
Understanding What You Read	Restating Main Idea	17 1, 21	____/3
Understanding Illustrations	Charts Line Graphs Bar Graphs	8, 9 19, 20 14, 15	____/6
Analyzing Ideas	Sequence Cause/Effect Inferences	13 3 6, 11	____/4
Building Vocabulary	Context Clues	10, 23	____/2
Evaluating Ideas	Values/Beliefs Incomplete Information Bias Reliable Sources	12, 24 7 25 22	____/5
		Total Correct	____/25

POST-TEST ANSWER KEY

1. **(5)** Choices **(1)** and **(3)** are too narrow; choice **(2)** is wrong because the government experiment was a failure; choice **(4)** is wrong because the deer caused no harm until the government removed the predators.

2. **(3)** Choices **(1)**, **(2)**, **(4)**, and **(5)** can be proved by measurement.

3. **(2)** Choice **(1)** is a cause, not an effect; choices **(3)** and **(4)** are effects of the large deer population; choice **(5)** is an effect of the lack of food.

4. **b** and **d**. The animal bones indicate that *Homo erectus* not only knew how to hunt but also ate meat, making choice (a) incorrect. Because they cooked in the cave, they probably lived there, making choice (c) incorrect. Since scientists found a group of bones, we know that *Homo erectus* probably lived in groups. Choice (e) is incorrect because the second sentence tells us the fossils are 300,000 years old.

5. **(3)** The first sentence of the paragraph tells you this. Choices **(1)**, **(2)**, **(4)**, and **(5)** are not suggested in the second paragraph.

6. **(3)**

7. **b** and **e**. You would need to know how much oxygen humans need and how much oxygen is produced by each plant.

8. **b** and **d**. According to the chart, iron and copper are both good conductors. Concrete is an average conductor.

9. **(4)** Styrofoam is the worst thermal conductor of the five choices and, therefore, the best insulator.

10. **(1)**

11. **(5)**

12. **(4)**

13. 2, 3, 1

14. **(4)**

15. **(5)** The graph shows the diameters of planets in thousands of kilometers.

16. **(1)** Jupiter is the largest planet on the graph.

17. **(3)**

18. **(1)** The passage states that radiocarbon shows signs of decay for 50,000 years. If it has stopped decaying, it is more than 50,000 years old.

19. **(5)**

20. **(3)**

21. **(4)** Choices **(1)**, **(2)**, and **(5)** are too narrow; they cover only part of the information. Choice **(3)** is never suggested in the passage.

22. **(1)** Choices **(3)**, **(4)**, and **(5)** are wrong because these individuals are not trained in environmental science. Choice **(2)** is incorrect as the first sentence states that the ozone layer began to be a concern in the early 1970s.

23. (3)

24. **(5)** People who believe in the miracle of St. Januarius probably believe that miracles are beyond science.

25. **(4)** A chemist is a man or woman of science.

ANSWER KEY

THE SCIENTIFIC METHOD

Fact and Opinion
Page 2
1. F

2. O

3. O

4. F The number of children who believe in Santa can be measured with a survey.

5. F

6. O

7. F The spacecraft's discoveries can be proved by researching the facts of the space mission.

8. O Whether something is beautiful cannot be tested. Beauty is judged according to personal values.

Everyday Hypotheses
Page 3
Your wording may vary, but your answers should contain the same information as the answers below.
1. The cold air is turning the plant yellow.

2. The watch is fast.

3. The neighbor will be back on Tuesday. He has not been home to collect his papers for four days, so he has three days of vacation left.

4. Most of the asbestos is located in the ceiling tiles, but some is located in the floor tiles as well.

Choosing Hypotheses
Page 4
1. (5) Choices (1), (3), and (4) are not true, based on the facts provided. Choice (2) is too broad; it states more than the facts suggest.

2. (3)

Making Hypotheses
Page 5
Your wording may vary, but your answers should contain the same information as the answers below.
1. There was at least one bad bulb on the string.

2. There was at least one other bad bulb on the string (so the lights didn't light even with the good spare) and/or the spare light bulb was bad.

3. The spare bulb was good.

4. The black bulb was bad.

5. There was at least one other bad bulb on the string.

6. To test lights on the first string, Angela should remove one bulb from the second string and replace it, one at a time, with the bulbs from the first string. This will tell her which bulb or bulbs are bad.

Errors in Experiments
Page 6
1. **no control group.** Chin-Hwa had no way to tell if the mice were drawn to the color green or if they just memorized which door the food was behind. A second set of mice with doors all the same color would, in fact, have learned to go to the second door.

2. **not enough subjects.** By trying the toothpaste on only two children, Imelda ignored the fact that one of the children might naturally be prone to cavities.

3. **subjects not similar.** Since the two-door car was lighter, it still might have slid on the road even with snow tires. On the other hand, the heavier truck probably would have gotten better traction than the car even without snow tires.

4. **conditions not kept the same.** Carmen washed one load of laundry in hot water and one load in cold. The hot water might have helped get the first load cleaner.

Review of the Scientific Method
Page 7
1. a
2. d
3. b
4. c
5. e

UNDERSTANDING WHAT YOU READ

Restating Facts
Page 8
1. (3) Choice (1) is incorrect because it says more than the original sentence says. Choices (2), (4), and (5) all state things that were not mentioned in the original sentence.

2. (1) Choice (2) is incorrect because the original sentence says nothing about plants dying, only growing. Choice (3) is incorrect because it mentions nothing about energy (the sun). Choice (4) states things not stated in the original sentence. Choice (5) discusses photosynthesis, which is not the same as the rate of growth.

3. (4) Choices (1), (2), and (3) are incorrect because they make claims that are not made in the original sentence. Choice (5) refers to life's drawbacks, while the original sentence refers to the drawbacks of nuclear power.

Restating Practice
Page 9
Your wording may vary, but your answers should contain the same information as the answers below.
1. All things are made of atoms.

2. The United States uses more gasoline than any other country in the world.

3. Scientists still don't know how the dinosaurs died.

4. The oldest living tree in the world is about 4,600 years old.

5. Studies show that alcoholism might be passed on from parents to children.

6. We know that porpoises are smart because they cooperate and protect each other under different circumstances.

7. Even though football players are bigger and faster today, football is still safer than it used to be.

8. Knowing how to use computers is a good skill in today's workplace.

Summarizing Facts
Page 10
1. (4) Choices (1), (2), and (3) are true, but they cover only part of the facts given.

2. (3) Choice (1) is true, but it covers only part of the facts given. Choice (2) makes a claim that is not mentioned in the facts. Choice (4) is implied by one of the facts, but it does not address all of the facts.

Summarizing Practice
Page 11
Your wording may vary, but answers should contain the same information as the answers below.
1. New products are often more expensive when they are first introduced.

2. Although computers are better than humans at some things, they cannot do anything they are not programmed to do.

3. As fossil fuels become more scarce, scientists are developing ways to replace them with other power sources.

Main Idea of a Paragraph
Pages 12-13
1. Fat can be very important to the survival of animals.

2. But while we know a great deal about *what* the brain does, we know far less about *how* it does it.

3. While birds and mammals are similar in some ways, their differences help them adapt to different environments.

4. Darwin's book was—and still is—a very controversial work.

5. Identical twins offer scientists a unique opportunity to compare the effects of heredity and environment.

Main Idea of a Passage
Pages 14–15
Your wording may vary, but your answers should contain the same information as the answers below.

1. Humans have always believed that language sets us apart from other animals.

2. A chimpanzee named Washoe learned to use language.

3. The experiments with Washoe have taught us that humans are not the only animals able to use language.

4. When a chimpanzee named Washoe learned to use language, it changed the way humans think of themselves.

5. **b** and **d**. Choices **a** and **e** are incorrect because they are not stated in the passage. Choice **c** is incorrect because the passage does not discuss the English language but rather language in general.

6. **(1)** Washoe's life in Africa is not mentioned in the passage.

7. **(3)**

UNDERSTANDING ILLUSTRATIONS

Diagrams
Pages 16–17
1. The title of the diagram is Water Supply System for the Town of Lamark.

2. The water pump is located inside the pumping station.

3. The gas is stored in an underground gas storage tank.

4. The gas would leak out of the tank and into the ground.

5. A gas leak could affect the people of Lamark if it leaked into the water supply. The gasoline would contaminate the town's drinking water.

Diagram Practice
Page 18
1. The title of the diagram is The Human Heart.

2. The upper chambers of the heart are called *auricles*.

3. When the blood leaves the left ventricle, it flows through the aorta to the body.

4. The blood flows through the pulmonary veins to the left auricle of the heart.

5. The blood gets fresh oxygen from the lungs.

Comparing Diagrams
Page 19
1. The title of the diagram is Cross Sections of Human Arteries (20× larger than actual).

2. The diagrams are called cross sections because they show a view that cuts across the artery.

3. Smaller. The title indicates that the arteries in the diagram are 20 times larger than actual human arteries. This is done so the details are easier to see.

4. The artery in Figure 1 leaves the most room for blood to flow, since it has no fatty deposits blocking it.

5. Because the fat builds up and clogs the walls of their patients' arteries.

Charts
Page 20
1. The title of the chart is Calories Burned During Different Activities.

2. The second and third columns show the calories burned per minute and the calories burned per hour.

3. Carrying a 130-pound load up stairs burns the most calories, 1,842 per hour.

4. During each minute spent weeding a garden, a person burns five calories.

5. Picking up around the house. Making beds burns 5.4 calories per minute, while picking up objects burns 5.9.

6. Cross-country running for one minute. Walking rapidly for two minutes burns 2 × 5.2 calories, or 10.4 calories. Cross-country running for one minute burns 10.6 calories.

Chart Practice
Page 21

1. According to Karl's measurements, the baseball and the large rock had the fastest falling time.

2. According to Karl's calculations, the baseball fell one one-hundredth of a second faster; it took 1.0 seconds to reach the ground while the metal pipe took 1.01 seconds. The metal pipe weighs 22 ounces—almost twice as much as the baseball.

3. The last five items on the list—the doll, the baseball, the pipe, the basketball, and the rock—all fell for about 1 second. Since they all fell at about the same rate, their different weights do not seem to have made a difference.

4. The paper airplane had the slowest falling time. The wind kept it up longer than the other items.

5. Karl's hypothesis was incorrect. In Karl's experiment, the lightest objects did take longest to fall. However, the baseball (12 oz.) fell at the same speed as the large rock (96 oz.). We can guess that wind resistance affected Karl's results. In fact, in a vacuum, all free-falling objects, regardless of weight, accelerate at the same rate.

Line Graphs
Pages 22-23

1. The horizontal axis shows the time of day.

2. The vertical axis shows the number of cars counted.

3. Traffic was heaviest at 9:00 A.M. and 6:00 P.M.

4. At 11:00 A.M., about 75 cars were counted. At 3:00 P.M., about 125 cars were counted. Your answers don't have to be exact, but they should be close to these figures.

5. Traffic was heaviest at times when people are driving to and from work. These high traffic periods are sometimes called rush hour.

6. The vertical axis shows the heart rate of Barry Smith.

7. The horizontal axis records the questions asked by the person who tested Barry.

8. Barry's heart rate stays at about 68 beats per minute during most of the questioning. This is average for a person sitting at rest.

9. His heart rate jumps to about 75 beats a minute.

10. The test results do not tell us for certain that Barry is lying. All they really tell us is that Barry became nervous when the tester asked certain questions.

Line Graph Practice
Page 24

1. T

2. F

3. T

4. F

5. F

Bar Graphs
Page 25

1. (5)

2. **b** and **d**. Choice **a** is incorrect because the graph shows that cows and horses—the two biggest animals—need very little sleep. Choice **c** is incorrect because cats are tame animals, and they need more sleep than many of the wild animals shown. Choice **e** is incorrect because the graph shows nothing about reptiles.

Bar Graph Practice
Pages 26–27

Your wording may vary, but your answers should contain the same information as the answers below.

1. According to the graph, humans had the shortest life expectancy around 700 B.C. in Greece.

2. 1910

3. About 25 years. In 1990, the average American had a life expectancy of 75 years. In 1910, the life expectancy was 50. 75 years − 50 years = 25 years.

4. According to the graph, human life expectancy has increased.

5. Better prenatal care, cleaner living conditions, and advances in surgery and vaccination all contribute to the longer life expectancy. Other reasons might include better working conditions and larger supplies of food.

6. The minke whale population was the largest, with 360,000 whales.

7. The minke whale population is largest today, with 300,000 whales.

8. The blue whales declined the most in number, from 200,000 to fewer than 20,000 whales.

9. Whale populations have decreased since 1650.

10. The graph tells us that the whale populations went down after commercial whaling began. The graph implies that whale hunting is responsible for the drop in population size.

ANALYZING IDEAS

Sequencing
Page 28

1. first. The engine starts after the spark plugs fire. The spark plugs must fire first.

2. in the meantime. They were trying to find a safe disposal method during the time waste was being produced.

3. after. Einstein made his speeches after the first atomic bomb was exploded.

Sequencing Practice
Page 29

1. Correct order: 5, 2, 1, 4, 3. Scientists were already splitting atoms by the 1930s; Einstein wrote to the president in 1939; the Manhattan Project began in 1942; the first bomb was exploded in 1945; and several weeks later, the United States dropped bombs on Hiroshima and Nagasaki.

Logical Sequence
Page 30

1. Logical order: b, a. The telescope had to be built before it was used.

2. Logical order: b, a, c. It couldn't have rained if the temperature was below freezing, and the ice couldn't have formed unless the highway was already wet.

3. Logical order: a, c, b. Neither the Lindbergh flight nor the Pan American flights could have occurred before the first plane was flown. It is logical to assume that someone (Lindbergh) had successfully crossed the Atlantic before passenger flights were introduced.

4. Logical order: c, b, a, d. Electricity was discovered before the light bulb; the light bulb existed when someone filled it with neon gas; someone invented neon lights before they were used on Hollywood Boulevard.

5. Logical order: **a, d, b, c.** Scientists must have known what carbon was before they discovered it in diamonds; if the engineers hadn't known diamonds are made of carbon, they could not have known to use carbon in artificial diamonds; and factories couldn't use artificial diamonds until they were invented.

Cause and Effect
Page 31
1. Cause: strong movements within the earth's crust occur beneath an ocean floor
Effect: huge sea waves called *tsunamis*

2. Cause: California's San Andreas Fault shifted
Effect: shaking was felt across the state, but damage was greatest in San Francisco

3. Cause: the ground moves
Effect: the pen or light ray on a seismograph makes a wavy line

4. Cause: scientists know to watch for these signs
Effect: scientists may be able to predict future earthquakes

Cause and Effect Practice
Pages 32–33
1. The molecules of the gas polymerized; they combined with one another.

2. It caused the gaskets to dissolve.

3. The gas had no effect on the Teflon gaskets.

4. 2, 1, 3, 5, 4. The gas polymerized; the polymer was discovered by Plunkett; scientists developed a way to produce Teflon; it was produced for the atomic bomb project; it was used on cookware.

5. (5) Plunkett's discovery did not cause the gas to polymerize.

6. (2) The passage is about the unusual way Teflon was discovered and developed. Choices **(1)** and **(4)** are incorrect because they imply the passage is about different ways to use Teflon. Choice **(3)** is incorrect because the passage is not about Roy Plunkett. Choice **(5)** is incorrect because, while Teflon was an accidental discovery, the passage is not about accidental discoveries in general.

Inferences
Page 34
1. that there was no UFO and that the man was drunk when he thought he saw it

2. You can infer four things about previous generations of computers:
   a. that they were less powerful than the new computers
   b. that they were slower than the new computers
   c. that they were less versatile than the new computers
   d. that they were more difficult to use than the new computers

3. that silver is used in the production of photographic film

4. that the experts believe controlling the weather could hurt our environment

Inference Practice
Page 35
Your wording may vary, but your answers should contain the same information as the answers below.
   1. that many of the scientists' suggestions are hard to believe

   2. that today's pills do not always release the correct amount of medication

   3. that in those days nobody realized all the ways they could be used

BUILDING VOCABULARY

Compound Words
Page 36
1. housework

2. overdose

3. wingspan

4. boathouse

5. underwater

6. Any five of the following are correct:
   powerboat, powerhouse, horsepower, horsefly, horseman, candlepower, candlelight, flytrap, houseboat, housecoat, overpower, overload, overstep, overcoat, overwork, manpower, manhole, workhorse, workhouse, workload, workman, waterpower, waterhole, undercoat, underwork, lighthouse, boatload

Defining Compound Words
Page 37
Your wording may vary, but your answers should contain the same information as the answers below.
1. headline—a line at the top, or head, of a newspaper story

2. overflow—extra; the amount that flows over the limit

3. commonplace—often seen or heard

4. drawback—disadvantage; a feature that would cause someone to draw back, or step away

5. landfill—a garbage dump; an area in which land is filled with garbage

6. widespread—widely or commonly used

7. outcry—objection; people crying out against something

8. eyesore—an ugly thing; something so ugly that it hurts the eyes when seen

9. overpowering—very strong; strong enough to have power over someone or something

10. worthwhile—worth someone's time

11. setback—something that reverses or sets back progress

Word Parts
Pages 38–39
1. a. bicycle—something with two wheels
   b. biped—something with two feet

2. a. prehistoric—before written history
   b. prenatal—before birth

3. a. exhale—breathe out
   b. extract—pull out

4. a. astronaut—a space traveler
   b. astrobiology—the study of living things in outer space

5. a. international—among nations
   b. interstellar—among the stars

6. a. herbicide—something that kills plants
   b. herbivorous—feeding on plants

7. a. rhinoceros—having a horn on the nose
   b. rhinoplasty—plastic surgery on the nose

8. a. unilingual—having one language
   b. unison—one sound

Context Clues
Page 40
1. (4)

2. (3)

3. (3)

4. (1)

Context Clues Practice
Page 41
Your wording may vary, but your answers should contain the same information as the answers below.
1. period—the time it takes a planet or comet to complete a full orbit, or return to the same spot

2. luminous—glowing, giving off light

3. astronomers—people who study outer space